Logan Hensley

Turbocharge Your Future

Revealing Interviews with the CEOs of eBay, Zappos, Sports
Authority, and Others About What Really Counts!

Logan Hensley

Copyright © 2014 Logan Hensley

Hensley, Logan.
Turbocharge your future : revealing interviews with the ceo's of ebay, zappos, sports authority, and others about what really counts / by Logan Hensley -1st ed.

p. ; cm.

ISBN-10: 1500458023
ISBN-13: 978-1500458027

First Edition

Printed in the United States of America

DEDICATION

I dedicate this book to my parents. I could not ask
for more supportive and loving people in my life.

Logan Hensley

CONTENTS

Logan Hensley

Introduction

You may wonder why I used the word "turbocharge" in my title. The purpose of a turbocharger is to increase performance in an engine. It compresses air and optimizes the combustion; therefore creating much more power. My book serves as an analogy for this technology; the air is knowledge available for students and this book compresses the information into usable advice that can help boost your performance in life.

I've always heard adults say that there were things they wish they had known when they were younger, so I decided to find out for myself what kind of "things" they were talking about. I figured that if I could be prepared for some of these obstacles, I'd be ahead of the game.

I began this project as a sophomore in high school when I was thinking about what I wanted to do with my life. It would be a few years before I applied to colleges, but I thought there might be a few extra things I could be doing in high school to prepare me for college, as well as the rest of my life.

I decided to contact people who reached the top of their respective fields to see what could come of our conversations. To my great surprise, everyone I asked agreed to talk to me.

This book consists of the conversations I had with these incredibly successful people. They include: the CEO of eBay; the CEO of Zappos; the CEO of Sports Authority; a former congressman; a retired three-star Navy admiral; a luxury retail builder; a female race car driver; the founder of a golf club company; an entrepreneur; and a Naval Academy graduate who had everything stacked against him at birth.

Each one of them has been kind enough to share some of the keys to his or her extraordinary success---and that's what I humbly present to you in this book.

What follows are excerpts of my conversations with ten individuals who have excelled in their own fields and on their own terms. What these people are talking about is not just theory--- their success is the proof of their statements.

Turbocharge Your Future

Logan Hensley

Interview Participants

Sandy Bauler,
Female Race Car driver; Motivational Speaker

Scotty Cameron,
Founder and CEO Scotty Cameron Putters

John Donahoe, CEO eBay

Michael Foss, CEO Sports Authority

Tony Hsieh, CEO Zappos

Frank Naliboff, CEO Dickenson Cameron
Construction

Hon. Ronald Packard, Former representative, California's 48th congressional district

Zerbin Singleton, U.S. Marine Corps Officer; Motivational Speaker

Robert J. "Rocky" Spane, Vice Admiral (ret), United States Navy; past Chairman Vanguard Airlines

Ted Vallas, Entrepreneur

Biographies in Alphabetical Order

Sandy Bauler

Sandy is a highly-skilled race car driver and motivational speaker. In 2000, she experienced a near-fatal crash while driving in a stock car race. She recovered and went back to racing, as well as to being an instructor at Rusty Wallace Racing Experience. In addition, she founded and serves as president of Driven2Dare, a driving school that teaches safe driving to teenagers and members of the military. Sandy has received national recognition for her cutting edge leadership in the areas of driving safety and responsibility.

Scotty Cameron

In the world of golf, everyone knows his name. He tirelessly worked on every single aspect of design and manufacturing to create what many say are the best putters in the world. A lot of pros, including Tiger Woods, have won numerous tournaments using Scotty Cameron putters. Mr. Cameron's genius doesn't stop with putters---it goes far beyond the world of golf club manufacturing.

John Donahoe

Mr. Donohoe is the president and CEO of eBay. Before becoming the president and CEO of eBay, he held the same positions at the international consulting firm of Bain and Company. Besides being a world-class business leader, Mr. Donahoe knows a thing or two about education. He graduated from Dartmouth and the Stanford Graduate School of Business.

Michael Foss

Mr. Foss is the CEO of Sports Authority. Sports Authority is a private company, which started as Gart Sports in 1928, and now has over 460 stores. Prior to becoming CEO of Sports Authority, Mr. Foss held significant positions in a variety of financial, retail, technology, and customer service companies including Circuit City and Petco Animal Supply. Mr. Foss is a graduate of the University of Washington, and the University of Michigan Stephen M. Ross School of Business.

Tony Hsieh

In 1995 Tony Hsieh, graduated from Harvard. In 1999 he sold a company that he co-founded, to Microsoft, for $265 million dollars. Mr. Hsieh is currently the CEO of Zappos.com. Zappos was purchased by Amazon.com for $1.2 billion in 2009, and Hsieh remains as CEO. Mr. Hsieh is also the co-founder of the investment firm Venture Frogs. In 2011 Mr. Hsieh joined the board of JetSuite, which is a jet charter company that flies private jets that are in the Very Light Jet category, and are extremely fuel efficient. Mr. Hsieh lives in Las Vegas, Nevada and is also currently involved in a revitalization project of downtown Vegas.

Frank Naliboff

Frank Naliboff has served as the Chief Executive Officer and President of Dickinson Cameron Construction (DCC) since co-founding the firm in 1994. Under Frank's leadership, DCC has become one of the nation's leading construction firms, serving high-end retail and restaurant clients which include: Apple, Calvin Klein, Cartier, Chanel, Fendi, Ralph Lauren, David

Yurman, Hermes, Burberry, Dolce & Gabbana, Tesla Motors, Tiffany & Co. and many other high-profile retail corporations. DCC sets the standard in high-end, luxury retail construction.

Hon. Ronald Packard

Mr. Packard is a former member of congress. He represented the 48th Congressional District. He earned a Doctor of Dental Medicine degree from the University of Oregon Dental School. Mr. Packard served in the Naval Dental Corps from 1957 to 1959. In terms of his political career, he served as a trustee in a school district, and subsequently was elected to city council, and subsequently became mayor. In terms of his congressional career, he lost a primary during his initial bid for a seat, but then launched a write-in campaign and won, becoming only the third person to be elected to congress via a write-in vote. He was re-elected to Congress eight times.

Zerbin Singleton

Zerbin is the most stunning example of overcoming diversity that I have ever seen. He was born to a drug-addicted mother, who struggled with her own challenges, which left Zerbin having to deal with a lot of situations at an early age that most people never have to confront, including homelessness. But, that was nowhere near enough to derail Zerbin. He ending up living with his aunt in Georgia, where he was able to concentrate on what he wanted to become in life. He passed that phase with flying colors.

Zerbin graduated from high school as class president and valedictorian, and won a highly-coveted appointment to the United States Naval Academy at Annapolis. However, in his senior year of high school, he was struck by a drunk driver and ended up not being physically qualified to attend the academy. Not deterred, he entered another college, and then gained entrance to the Naval Academy a year later. He became a star at the academy, both on the football field and off. He earned the rank of Brigade Commander, making him the highest ranking midshipman at the academy. Upon graduation, he accepted a commission into the United States Marine Corps. He is the recipient of the Disney Spirit Award; and the FedEx Orange Bowl Courage Award and was called "the most inspirational and courageous collegiate football player in the nation." Zerbin has appeared on all major and cable television networks, and continues to serve his country as a Marine Officer.

Admiral Robert J. "Rocky" Spane

Admiral Spane spent 35 years in the United States Navy, retiring as a three-star Vice Admiral, Commander of Naval Air Forces, Pacific. During his career, Admiral Spane held a variety of significant positions, yet he says his favorite was when he served as skipper of the USS Enterprise aircraft carrier. Following his naval career, Mr. Spane held numerous positions from Chairman of the San Diego Unified Port District, to Chairman of Vanguard Airlines. Admiral Spane's vast leadership experience is widely recognized and his advice is frequently sought by companies, boards, as well as congressional committees.

Ted Vallas

It's hard to think of anything that Mr. Vallas has not done. He was a star athlete in high school; a minor-league baseball pitcher; served during

World War II; developed golf courses and resorts all over the world; was the president of a TV station; founded aviation companies; founded two airlines; and so much more. Mr. Vallas has wisdom that is constantly sought by everyone from friends and family, to corporate boards.

Behind the Scenes

When I started this project nearly two years ago, I thought I was going to meet with successful people, conduct interviews, and then perhaps compile them into a book. Little did I know I would come away with so much more.

In this section of the book, I'd like to share some of the unique experiences I had with each of the participants I was fortunate enough to interview.

Scotty Cameron

When I set up my interview with Scotty Cameron, he told me to meet him at his house. I showed up, and the first thing he said to me was, "how much time do you have?" I told him I had as much time as he did. He knew beforehand that I was a car guy, so he decided to take me for a ride in his Mercedes SLS AMG. This is a true supercar, it is faster than almost any Ferrari or Lamborghini. We first went to get lunch at a resort located in Rancho Santa Fe, California. I conducted my interview at the restaurant. After lunch, he let me drive one of his prized possessions, a 1972 Chevelle SS. After this ride, he took me on a tour of his workshop/office.

Externally, this building looked like any other in the area, but the interior looked like the Willy Wonka chocolate factory of golf. He showed me where he specifically designs putters, as well as where he uses an entire studio to custom fit and tune putters for individuals. This experience was a once-in-a-lifetime opportunity and amazed me.

Zerbin Singleton

When you read Zerbin Singleton's bio and interview answers, you'll quickly see what an exceptional and inspirational person he is. But, I found out so much more about him than I ever thought would be possible. He offered to pick me up and take me to the flight line at Camp Pendleton (a Marine base in San Diego County). He let me get inside of a couple of the helicopters which was an awesome experience. On a side note, he offered to come to my gym and lift weights with me at another time. Both he and I are about the same size, but he is by far the strongest pound for pound person I have ever lifted with. I was astonished and tried my best to keep up but it wasn't even close.

John Donahoe

` The interview process with Mr. Donahoe was different from the others. His assistant and I worked on scheduling a phone interview. It took a while, but eventually she told me "he has 2:45-3:15 p.m. free in three weeks." It was astonishing to find out that someone literally has their schedule booked in 15 minute increments weeks in advance.

Admiral Spane

I met Admiral Spane at an event at Palomar-McClellan Airport. When I first had an opportunity to speak to him, I had no idea about the rank or position he had achieved in the military. After I talked to him, my dad told me about his background and I was amazed. I sought out his phone number and gave him a call. I asked if I could interview him for my book, and he generously accepted. I asked if I could meet him close to where he lived on Coronado Island to (One: because I didn't want him to have to drive a long way, and Two: because Coronado is such a beautiful place). We had lunch at a coastal café and I was intrigued by all of the knowledge and advice he had to offer.

Congressman Packard

Before meeting Congressman Packard, I had never met anyone with freeways and streets named after him. As I was driving to our interview location, I actually transited a street named after him! Speaking to someone who was re-elected to congress EIGHT times was astounding.

Ted Vallas

Being able to interview Mr. Vallas was a true gift. I was blown away. He was a Naval gunner in World War II, a professional baseball player, the president of a TV station, and an incredibly successful entrepreneur. Each one of these pursuits could stand alone as an extraordinary accomplishment.

Frank Naliboff

One of Mr. Naliboff's employees is a close family friend of ours, and that's how I was able to get an introduction to him. I knew that he worked in high-end retail construction, but had not idea of the success his company had achieved and the companies who trusted him to build their retail locations. Some of the companies that trust him to build their spectacular retail locations include Apple, Tesla Motors, Nordstrom, Mont Blanc,

Calvin Klein, Giorgio Armani, Adidas, and countless more. Mr. Naliboff is an approachable and generous person, and the magnitude of his clientele is staggering.

Sandy Bauler

Mrs. Bauler and I connected as fellow car enthusiasts, similar to the way I connected with Scotty Cameron. We met at a restaurant halfway from both of our hometowns. Aside from the interview, we talked for an hour and a half solely about cars and racing. Our conversation began with her telling me about the ins and outs of the world of racing and ended with our discussing perspectives on different street cars' capabilities. It was an absolute pleasure to converse with this amazing woman, and I learned so much---about life and about cars!

Michael Foss

Mr. Foss's perspectives on business and success are profound. He literally had a well thought out and impressive philosophy on every subject I brought up. He told me how at one point in his career, he left a successful position for a much more difficult one --- just for the sake of a challenge. I do not know many people who would take such a risk, and I find it refreshing to discover that there are people as smart, spontaneous, and insightful as Mr. Foss at the top echelons of the business world.

Tony Hsieh

I am most proud of securing the interview with Mr. Hsieh. It was the biggest long-shot I attempted, as I had no previous connection to him or his company. I simply called the Zappos 800 number and asked for Mr. Hsieh. I left a voicemail with his assistant and I later found out that she had expeditiously relayed my message to him. She got back in touch with me and told me to send her the questions via e-mail. I was stunned when I subsequently received a response directly from Mr. Hsieh. It was hard to believe that a person at his level would take the time to respond to a teenager's request for an interview. I learned a lot about him from that alone.

Reading Tips

If you have only a short time to glance through this book, you can simply read the boxed text to get some of the highlights. I'm confident you'll want to read the rest when time permits.

In addition, I've included a page at the end of each section where you can write down what you got out of the answers, and how you can use that insight to help shape your future.

Logan Hensley

QUESTION 1

What can high school and college students do now to help prepare and distinguish themselves later in a competitive job market?

Tony Hsieh, *CEO, Zappos:*

Spend more time doing stuff that's outside your comfort zone. Meet people from different backgrounds. Start a club. Take more risks.

John Donahoe, *President and CEO, eBay:*

The first thing that comes to my mind is to discover and pursue your passion, because my observation is that people do their best when they're doing things they love... Figuring out your passion is hard, and you never stop doing it...but you figure it out by living life and trying different things.

Number two is embrace learning. Michael Jordan and Kobe Bryant redefined basketball, and everyone around them will tell you they're the two hardest workers in their generation. Michael Jordan came in and he didn't just depend on being able to shoot a jump shot and dunk. He worked on his defense, team work, and his passing. He had clarity... And he wasn't afraid to admit, "I wanted to get better here." And he worked on it...

Kobe Bryant works on every step that he likes to use in a game; every step and move. So, when he get[s] to the game, it feels natural. He breaks it down and he works harder.

... I really think the most successful people that I know generally, have found what they love to do; I call that your passion. And they are deeply committed to their own personal growth.

Three: teamwork... Find experiences and environments where you have to be part of the key. And ideally, part of the key is that people are just like you. Because in the whole world, you have to be comfortable working with other people different than you to get stuff done. Make sure you reach out to people beyond that and learn how to get some experience with people who think differently than you, and see if you can do it in a context where you have a shared goal.

Frank Naliboff, *Luxury Retail Builder:*

Think about what your actions are today, and...what will be hanging around your neck five years and ten years from now. What a lot of kids don't understand is the things they do in social media have consequences, the things they do as a result of peer pressure have consequences, and so from a leadership standpoint, the leaders of today are the guys who don't follow, they set their own course, and sometimes that's difficult, especially when you're in high school when you have peer pressure, because it's so tough...Some of those decisions will affect your work in the classroom, but more importantly, they're going to affect your work in life, that's just the way it is.

Sandy Bauler, *Race Car Driver:*

Exploring everything that they like and by participating. Volunteering, jobs, internships: just get out there and do it because you don't know what you don't know. There are so many things out there that you don't even know exist. I would say that most of the jobs I've gotten, all the opportunities I've gotten, were because I was out in the community doing something. Jobs came to me. Opportunities have come to me. I would never have found them had I not been out there.

Scotty Cameron, *Founder & CEO of Scotty Cameron Putters:*

Do something you enjoy or you think you are going to enjoy.

Ted Vallas, *Entrepreneur:*

Try as soon as possible to get at what your true interests are... Whether it's business, whether it's government, whatever it is. And then try during the period of time to avail yourself to that industry; at least to do a little on it… Do you feel it will hold your interest for a long time or a short period of time?

Michael Foss, *CEO, Sports Authority:*

The more you can get out and do different kinds of jobs to demonstrate that you can work in a team-oriented environment, that you have the right kind of productivity, that you are continually looking – all that stuff would help.

Hon. Ronald Packard, *Former Congressman:*

Having a good education is crucial. Even people who are highly educated, who have a degree, still find it difficult to get work. They naturally have an advantage over those who don't get a high school or college education, or those who don't pursue education. In a tough job market like we have right now, there's no question that an education will be an advantage. It doesn't guarantee you work; it certainly doesn't guarantee you work in a field that you graduated in. But in most cases it will, and if you're patient, it will lead you to opportunities that will allow you to work in the area that you studied, that you're interested in, that you are eager to get involved with.

1 Minute Drill

Take no more than 1 minute to write down what stuck with you

from the previous answers...ready...GO

_____

_____

_____

_____

_____

_____

_____

_____

_____

_____

_____

_____

_____

_____

_____

_____

_____

Logan Hensley

QUESTION 2

What was your biggest failure, and what did you learn from it?

Michael Foss, *CEO, Sports Authority*:

My biggest failures have been acquisitions that I've [made]. I've done, I don't know, about 30 acquisitions in my career that didn't go as expected. I bought a company in Spain for $90 million...and almost from the minute we bought the company the business headed south. So we had to go in and do some pretty nasty restructuring work to get the thing turned around. That wasn't work we intended to do... I couldn't predict it as well as I should have. You'll make wrong decisions, but at the end of the day, it's how quickly you recognize a wrong decision and then what steps do you take to fix [it].

... That's why you have to be really objective. Because it's not that you made the wrong decision; where somebody gets into trouble is where you make the wrong decision and you're in denial for a long time. So if you made the wrong decision or something went wrong...recognizing it quickly and then taking proactive steps to address it is what turns what could be problems into potential successes.

John Donahoe, *CEO, eBay*:

In 1992, I made a really big deal and the whole organization thought we didn't make any progress, because two years later, I talked bolder than I [could] act, than I [could] deliver. In eBay, I had certain instincts that I thought were right, but I was called wrong. I didn't really understand about serving customers, so I didn't listen to my instinct. [I thought,] "I don't know. I don't really understand. They must be right." And it turned out [that] following other people's recommendations was really bad, because I thought I wasn't right. So, it was about...following my instinct[s].

Zerbin Singleton, *U.S. Marine Corps Officer,* *Motivational Speaker:*

I can name a couple: At the [Naval] Academy in my freshman year, I got an Honor Offense for cheating on a military test. So that was a pretty big setback. It wasn't my character. It was just that I felt I had to study for other stuff more important than that...[The result was that a] lot of people lost confidence in me. But I merely used that as a teaching point and learning point, so when I became Brigade Commander at the Naval Academy, it was something that came up in one of the many interviews... [The] point was that you could fail but still do great things.

Finally, I always wanted to fly jets... I used to help the chief, our ROTC instructor, with his computer and things and he asked me where I was looking to go to college. And I said, "The Air Force Academy." He was like, "Why not the Naval Academy?" I was like, "Because I want to fly." I didn't know the Navy flew... And he was like, "Would you rather land on land or would you rather land on a carrier, pitch black at night, that tips from side to side?" And I'm pretty adventurous and I was like, "That sounds pretty cool..." [But] in flight school, I just didn't do well enough to get jets. I was disappointed about that.

Ted Vallas, *Entrepreneur:*

My biggest failure was trusting [the] wrong people...maybe over-trusting some people. I had people steal from me. An insurance agent at a very crucial time in the aviation business, in which insurance is a must, was putting all the premiums in his pocket instead of turning them over to the insurance company; [he was] falsifying insurance documents... And I received a call after being a successful bidder on three new government contracts. The person who had lost the contract questioned the insurance area and sure enough it was discovered. The [insurance agent] went to jail, but at the time I lost those contracts. I also had other contracts that were multi-million dollar contracts that I could not get reinsured in a timely manner unless I subbed out or paid other people to run all of those contracts for me.

And that's a period of time [when] you couldn't [subcontract to other people] because it took at least three months to make your initial contact for your insurance, and they had what they called re-insurers. Nobody insures totally... So to get substitute service for all the contracts I had at the time, I would have had to pay out multi-millions. So we sold the certificate; any contracts that we had, we had to spin-off to other people.

Sandy Bauler, *Race Car Driver:*

...Failure is only temporary. It doesn't define who I am. And someone told me a long time ago that it takes 99 No's to get a Yes. And that's kind of what I go for. So when people say, oh you really failed---well, I say obviously that didn't work, let's do something else. So to say which is your biggest failure? I don't know – I've had so many. You know, from making bad decisions in school to marriages.

Scotty Cameron, *Founder & CEO of Scotty Cameron Putters:*

My biggest failure, gosh, I always think when things go wrong and you think that you failed, it's always an opportunity to learn from your mistakes and to do it better. So I've always thought – knock on wood – when something hits me so hard as to think it's a failure, I've always been able to turn that and make it a positive. I haven't had a whole lot of those. It's surrounding yourself with friends and good people and asking the opinion of people who have been in those positions. But, I just look at things as an opportunity.

Tony Hsieh, *CEO, Zappos*:

I haven't been able to figure out how to get enough sleep and exercise and hang out with friends and work on everything I need to do for Zappos and the Downtown Project. So generally sleep and exercise end up losing out, which I know is not healthy for the long term.

Frank Naliboff, *Luxury Retail Builder:*

Where I failed miserably was in my ability to manage people. I failed and failed and failed, it was such a hard learning process because it took me forever to realize that as a business owner, the folks that work for me, I have to give them a safe place to work...but I can't be their friend.

So my failure wasn't a single event, my failure was ten years, fifteen years of failing every day at being a good manager. And I wasn't doing them any favors, I was allowing mediocre behavior. Not only was it bad for the business, it was bad for them. And so to realize it was my defining moment and I don't know if there was a training that I could have done ten years prior to get me better at doing it, I think maybe it's just one of those things you just had to learn but I'm happy I did.

1 Minute Drill

Take no more than 1 minute to write down what stuck with you

from the previous answers...ready...GO

_____

_____

_____

_____

_____

_____

_____

_____

_____

_____

_____

_____

_____

_____

_____

_____

Logan Hensley

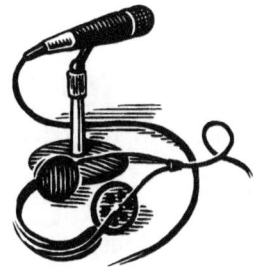

QUESTION 3

What are some of the best predictors of success?

Admiral Robert J. "Rocky" Spane, *U.S. Navy Vice Admiral (ret); past Chairman, Vanguard Airlines:*

In the big philosophical point of view, what military officers bring to the table that a business person might not have, in some sense, is honesty, integrity, and accountability. If you want to be successful, you should work on those kinds of things. Like the boy scout motto: "We don't lie, cheat or steal." We take responsibility for what we do and what we don't do. And we don't lie our way out of it...

You can be helpful if you join some of the military units that are in the high school, but I don't think that makes a real difference... The real principle idea is honesty and integrity.

Michael Foss, *CEO, Sports Authority*:

I think it's intelligence. I think it's a willingness to take a level of risk; it's having some self-confidence to be able to go and challenge some things. I think all those are pretty critical skills, but probably the most fundamental is the ability to work well with other people.

…You look for things that differentiate them. Grades are a really important part of that, but it's only one part of many things. Your resume, which is just a summary about you, has to be able to stand out in some way, shape or form or you'll never get to that interview process. So grades are a piece, but only one piece of many that would help you get to that level.

The broader the courses you take will be beneficial and your grades will be beneficial. The more you can get out and do different kinds of jobs to demonstrate that you can work in a team-oriented environment, that you have the right kind of productivity, that you are continually looking – all that stuff would appear. If I am looking at your resume, it would help me believe that you would be a real strong candidate for an open position that we have.

The more diversity you can show in terms of things you've excelled at: volunteer work is always great, because you'll like that about a person, and it says they have a conscience, a social or a moral compass that is healthy and good. The more you can do…whether it is co-op assignments or internships or working in a diversity of different environments, whether volunteer work or for pay, I think would be helpful.

Frank Naliboff, *Luxury Retail Builder:*

Hard work. It's a very intangible thing, but it's a very easy thing for me to spot. And I don't mean looking like you work hard, I mean literally working hard. It's not always about time, it's always about effort. What did you do today to make this company, or this situation, or this organization better? What did you do to make it progress? I believe it's a predictor of peoples' outside influence. They have churches and youth organizations and all those kinds of things that they go to outside of work and to me it's really easy to say, yep, I bet that person donates to their community and does all those kinds of things, I can see it.

Scotty Cameron, *Founder & CEO of Scotty Cameron Putters:*

When I look at young juniors and titles and look at signing some of these younger pros, like Tiger Woods, you always have to look at their parents. How focused, how driven are they? Is school the end-all? It's not. But it's definitely something…you look at as part of the whole package. I think the whole package is your background, your parents, your schooling and your drive.

So, to find kids with a work ethic is huge. That's my biggest problem as an employer…finding people with a work ethic of wanting to work hard. Everybody wants to make the big bucks and not work hard, but when you find a great work ethic, it's so valuable.

Hon. Ronald Packard, *Former Congressman:*

I think there are several things that...qualify a person to be a good elected official. First: don't get pigeonholed into very narrow issues. That happens in local government a lot.

[Second]... I think, you have to be willing and have the time to do your homework.

[Third]... I think that leadership is a huge part of serving. You need to be willing and able to be a leader, and be willing to take leadership responsibility and a leadership role in the decision-making process. Also, you need to be willing to divide your time appropriately.

It takes time to serve in public office, and you still need to spend time with your children, with your husband, your wife, your family. You need to make sure you have time to devote to your office, but also maintain other very important priorities in your life. The last thing you'll want is you run for public office and then lose your family.

Ted Vallas, *Entrepreneur.*

Definitely not aptitude tests! A lot of companies use aptitude tests. I personally did a study in aptitude testing and I was told that I was musically inclined, as an example. I couldn't even spell music, let alone perform it!

And not...grades... They don't want just a talented student... Anybody that's always at the top of the class is a student more than they are people absorbing things.

1 Minute Drill

Take no more than 1 minute to write down what stuck with you from
the previous answers...ready...GO

_____

_____

_____

_____

_____

_____

_____

_____

_____

_____

_____

_____

_____

_____

_____

_____

_____

QUESTION 4

What's the best way to prepare for the work environment? What makes a good employee?

Scotty Cameron, *Founder & CEO of Scotty Cameron Putters:*

Put yourself in the right position, so if you want to be a car guy, then you hang with car guys. If you want to be a car guy, you don't hang with tennis guys. You don't hang with the golf guys if you're a car guy.

Michael Foss, *CEO, Sports Authority:*

Working in many different job environments or volunteer environments will give you great experience because you're going to find, all throughout your career, really good managers and really bad managers...If you're smart...you're going to learn from all of them...What was it about that boss that made him great?... You try to find what are the things that made him successful...and incorporate that into how you approach your job.

So there have been a hundred different executives who have really helped influence me and my behavior and how I approach things. And I would say two-thirds of them were people I really admired, and a third of them were people I didn't admire. I learned from both.

Frank Naliboff, *Luxury Retail Builder:*

For me, what I'm trying to get through to anybody is, if what you're doing doesn't work, try something new, try it again, and keep trying until it works. That's the philosophy that I use. Every day, I'm working under schedules of trying to build buildings for people whose most important thing is to get the building done. So, they can get the store open and start selling stuff. If what I'm doing on that particular day isn't working to progress the project I'll try something new and for me, my part of dreaming big is to say hey wait a minute, has anybody ever thought about doing it this way? It's the asking of the questions that's important. For me, as a business owner, I want to always dream big. Most importantly for my employees, I want them to do it too.

Ted Vallas, *Entrepreneur.*

Try and avoid the wrong associates. Take a good look at them. Do you want to be like them or do you want to be better than them? If you want to be better than them, stay away from them.

1 Minute Drill

Take no more than 1 minute to write down what stuck with you from
the previous answers...ready...GO

_____

_____

_____

_____

_____

_____

_____

_____

_____

_____

_____

_____

_____

_____

_____

_____

QUESTION 5

Was there a pivotal event or experience that put you on a path to success?

Zerbin Singleton, *U.S. Marine Corps Officer;*
Motivational Speaker.

I think the biggest thing is my faith - my faith in God. And my faith that I can do all things through Him. But all the events in my life have set me up to be the person I am, the good and the bad...

I came from a single parent home, living with my mother who was addicted to drugs. At times we were homeless, seeing domestic violence, so you get beat a lot...When my mother was in jail, I moved to Georgia where I lived with my cousins... In fifth grade, I realized I wanted to be an astronaut. I researched the astronaut basic requirements, and learned that you have to have a bachelor of science [degree]. That means you have to go to college, and my parents [didn't] have money to send me to college. So, I knew I was going to have to do something to get to college, whether it was academics or athletics. I really applied myself...meaning I lived my life trying to be the best of everything that I [could] be... Eventually, I overcame all that and became the man I am today.

Sandy Bauler, *Race Car Driver:*

There are actually two that were monumental for me. The first one was actually the loss of my child, and that took me a long time. That really led me into a lot of soul searching on who I was and what I needed to do and why was I here.

Then the other one was when I had my wreck in 2000. I was almost killed racing, and it was just a turning point... I was racing and a guy took me out... He did the PIT maneuver, and I was probably in fourth at that point... I couldn't really save it. I was kind of going towards the wall and so I thought, 'I'm just going to stop,' and then my spotter told me, "Okay; after the last place car, go ahead, start it back up and go." So I had the clutch pushed in, but the guy who was driving off the nose of his car drove in full speed and the car caved in around me and shoved my leg through my pelvis because my leg was straight. Yeah, I didn't feel it. I didn't feel my legs.

I just wanted to be this phenomenal, everybody-knew racer. But I had four kids, a family, had a regular job, had a business, you know. How can you be team mom and just try to juggle all that? And that whole incident…when you almost die and they tell you you're never going to walk again… How do you turn that around and overcome that? And how do you re-focus on overcoming those odds?

It took me about six months to even know whether I would walk again or not. And the whole time my doctor kept saying, 'Don't plan on it,' but I had good people in my life and they started planning for me to race with hands, like the Indy car-drivers do. So they were all trying to figure out how to make Sandy race again, you know, that type of thing, because I try to be the driving force but sometimes you're not.

At one point I know I had to make a decision about whether I wanted to live or not. You know, where I knew I had to consciously make that choice. And I think once you do, then you start looking at who really is there for you and who really isn't, and what is my purpose? I think that is when my volunteer work became huge. And it took me in a whole different direction as a teacher; I teach now. I teach racing and I teach entrepreneur classes. I don't like school, and now I'm teaching. So you know all those things happened and I worked hard overcoming that and coming to the realization that that wasn't the direction I needed to go.

Michael Foss, *CEO Sports Authority.*

Well, I've had a good career. I've been lucky in many situations. I've had a couple of very courageous bosses who put me in situations that, frankly, I wasn't qualified for and they knew it, but their view was in six months I could train you in what you don't know, but in six months you would be far better because of your inherent capabilities, or your intellect or your knowledge or your drive, than any of the other candidates.

Scotty Cameron, *Founder & CEO of Scotty Cameron Putters:*

When I was going through high school, I wanted to buy, what at that time was called, a moped. I was 15½ and I just wanted an odd job to help pay for that moped. I got this odd job and it was working at this Wienerschnitzel [restaurant] – a hot dog deal. I worked there for a night. I went in the next day and talked to the manager. After one night, at 15½ years old, I said, "This is not for me." He goes, "How would you know? You've only worked here one night." I said, "I know. I don't want to waste your time or mine. I'm done." He says, "If you quit now, you'll be a quitter for the rest of your life." And that one stuck with me, because I wasn't a quitter. I just knew what I wanted and didn't want.

Frank Naliboff, *Luxury Retail Builder:*

I started out at the lower level as an engineer, and I was out on the job sites, then I got a chance to come in the office, and the first six months of my experience in the office I realized that I had large ambitions and I knew that I was going to hit this wall because there was another fellow there, and I knew he was my impediment to being where I wanted to be...I started to resent him... [Then] a guy I knew from college approached me...he said, "hey, I'm looking for a general manager, a guy to run my back office because I want to go out and do work." For me, being an entrepreneur at heart, the light bulb went on and I got a chance to do my own thing. That was the day I knew I was an entrepreneur...for me that was the turning point... That business morphed into this business, it was a precursor for this company.

Logan Hensley

1 Minute Drill

Take no more than 1 minute to write down what stuck with you from the previous answers...ready...GO

_____

_____

_____

_____

_____

_____

_____

_____

_____

_____

_____

_____

_____

_____

_____

_____

_____

_____

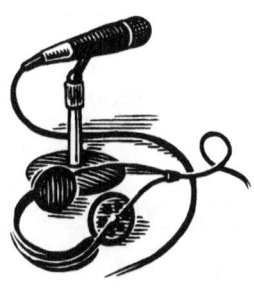

QUESTION 6

**If you were to change something about your high
school or college experience, what would it be?
What would you tell today's students to do
differently?**

Ted Vallas, *Entrepreneur.*

Have less fun. Be as serious as you can, because that's an education that is offered to you, and in college, unlike high school, it's up to you, and you, yourself, to absorb all you can.

Scotty Cameron, *Founder & CEO of Scotty Cameron Putters:*

I thought I had an idea of what I wanted to do – I wanted to be in the golf business. And…people kept saying, "You can't do that. Everybody wants to be a golf pro." I kind of caved, and looked for other avenues outside of high school to do something, but I finally came back to the golf business. When they said I couldn't, I always asked, "Why not?" So don't listen to the naysayers. Believe in your dream.

Sandy Bauler, *Race Car Driver:*

I kind of just…went through school just taking this and taking that and felt like I didn't really have much of a direction. Luckily, I went more with the passion and then doing the community work; just getting out there, working and doing things is kind of how things just transpired… Follow…your passion. I think that when you find out what drives you; everything else comes along.

1 Minute Drill

Take no more than 1 minute to write down what stuck with you from
the previous answers...ready...GO

_____

_____

_____

_____

_____

_____

_____

_____

_____

_____

_____

_____

_____

_____

_____

_____

_____

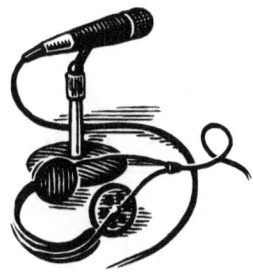

QUESTION 7

What is the most significant role a parent can play in a high school or college student's life?

Michael Foss, *CEO Sports Authority*:

I think parents are critical. Especially as you're just entering into college or just entering into the work environment, you're going to see lots of things you've never been involved in before and you know you'll need people to help you out, walk you through that, or what do you do or how do you react when you have a challenge with a co-worker or you don't think your boss likes you. I mean, all those will be new experiences for you.

Admiral Robert J. "Rocky" Spane, *U.S. Navy Vice Admiral (ret); past Chairman, Vanguard Airlines*:

Setting the example, of course. I'm 72 years old, and my dad died 20 years ago. But there's not a day that goes by that I don't think about him and think about what he would want me to do. So, you never get over being a child. And once you [have] children, you never get over being the parent. So, you are going to set an example for your children.

Ted Vallas, *Entrepreneur.*

[Maintain] constant contact with [your] child; I think that is very basic. And be honest with [your] parents [even] if you feel like…that isn't what you really want to do; be honest with them.

1 Minute Drill

Take no more than 1 minute to write down what stuck with you from
the previous answers...ready...GO

_____

_____

_____

_____

_____

_____

_____

_____

_____

_____

_____

_____

_____

_____

_____

_____

_____

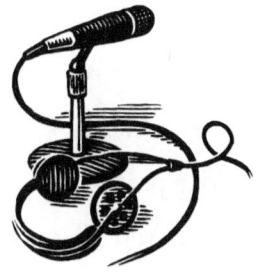

QUESTION 8

If you had one minute to give a message to a football stadium filled with high school and college students, what would the message be?

John Donahoe, *CEO, eBay:*

Embrace learning and treat life as a journey, not a destination. Learn in classroom, outside the classroom, and with your friends. Understand that life is a long journey. Your parents are still learning. I'm still learning about life. And if you treat it that way, you can never reach the failing line.

Admiral Robert J. "Rocky" Spane, *U.S. Navy Vice Admiral (ret); past Chairman, Vanguard Airlines:*

Take responsibility and accountability of your actions. And if you lie, cheat or steal, you're not the person that I want to be around. Have passion for what you do. It sounds pretty simple-minded, but it's hard to find people like that.

Hon. Ronald Packard, *Former Congressman:*

One item is not going to make or break a person in college or out of college. I would encourage them to develop within their whole soul, that Christian-Judeo concept of what kind of a good person we have to be: being honest...being loyal to your family, your wife, your husband, your job, and your community. That would certainly be one of the foremost parts of what I would encourage every person to try to become. Just become a very, very decent person. With their lifestyle, reflect what is important to them. Live that kind of lifestyle and become that kind of person. The decency of the human being qualifies a person to succeed.

[Second], I would certainly encourage...getting a good education as much as I can, because it will be a blessing to them throughout their life. They may not go in to their field of study, but a good broad education is very valuable, and it enhances specific goals in your educational pursuits.

[Third], develop an attitude of determination. Set goals, and then work with all your heart for achieving those goals, and never give up on your goals---good goals. Important and proper goals... You could succeed in virtually anything you want to do if you are willing to put in what it takes... To be a winner, you have to be willing to do the things that losers won't do.

Michael Foss, *CEO, Sports Authority*:

Challenge everything. You can dream as high as you want to dream, but you've got to be able and willing to work at it. Keep learning, keep thinking of building blocks; keep setting a vision of what you want to do for right now, what types of skills you need to be able to do that and keep, especially early in your career, getting those building blocks or skills.

...Think long term, think broadly; figure out how you can become an amazing leader and get people to want to work for you and [who] want you to provide leadership to them. Anything you can do along that line will be phenomenal. Keep getting as diverse a set of experiences as you can, because you'll keep getting better and better and better.

And finally, watch people. Learn from people. Learn from everybody.

Frank Naliboff, *Luxury Retail Builder:*

I guess for me, my disappointment in what I see now is a lack of true commitment by younger folks in being good citizens. I think we have become a society of thinking that people are going to hand us everything and that's frustrating for me. I would like to tell people that the course in their life can't be set by the government, it can't be set by parents, it can't be set by anybody, it has to be set by them. And to change that, they literally have to want to change it. They have to stop waiting for someone to tell them what to do, they have to say this is what I want, and go do it. In this country you can do whatever it is you set your mind to.

Sandy Bauler, *Race Car Driver:*

You can't change the whole world, but it's your job to change your corner of it. And you can do that when you go out and follow what your heart tells you to do. Because I think that so many people tell you what you should be doing, and if it's not a bad thing, then I think you should follow that because that is what you're supposed to do.

Scotty Cameron, *Founder & CEO of Scotty Cameron Putters:*

Avoid the naysayers. Everybody wants to tell you why you can't or why you shouldn't. I ran into those a long time ago... I wanted a high-end putter market; I wanted the best. That took money. A guy went into a store and my putters were $300 and the average putter was $100. I heard many times from the people that you'll be out of business in six months; you're out of your mind. How do you even know the top companies can afford that price mark? "You're crazy, you shouldn't do it. You'll be out of business." If I had listened to those naysayers, I would never have followed the dream.

The naysayers – those people who say you can't: stay away from them. You can do anything if you believe in it. Run from the naysayers.

Zerbin Singleton, *U.S. Marine Corps Officer,* *Motivational Speaker:*

Play every minute of your life like it's your last, whether you're on or off the field. Always give a hundred percent of your effort. You'll never know who is watching. You'll never know what opportunity you're in until you're out of it, then it might be too late. And always help the next person out whether they've done good or bad for you.

Ok, now after having finished the book, go back to your 1 Minute Drills and on this page, write down **THREE** things that you can commit to doing. This is your chance to apply the wisdom of some of the most successful people around---think about what a difference it can make if you do even just a few things that they recommend. . .

_____

_____

_____

_____

_____

_____

_____

_____

_____

_____

_____

_____

_____

_____

_____

_____

_____

So Where Do We Go From Here?

This has been quite a journey. I spent over a year seeking out highly-accomplished people who would be willing to talk to a teenager about success in life after high school and college. I'm honored and humbled by the fact that each one of them said "yes," and fit our meeting into their busy schedules that, in some instances, were booked in 15-minute increments months in advance. The first lesson I learned was that most extremely successful people have mastered the art of scheduling their time. I've got a long way to go in that area, but at least now I know what the goal is.

Second, I learned that the old adage of "ask and ye shall receive" rings true. Who would have thought that a three-star admiral, a CEO, or a race car driver would sit down with me, a teenager, for a two-hour lunch and tell me what they think really counts in life?

So, where do we go from here? If you're like me, we'll likely be going on a similar journey. I'll do my best to follow the advice that these world-class high achievers have passed on to me. But, I know that realistically, because of human nature, or maybe just my nature, that I'll likely fall short.

No one is perfect, and learning from failure is sometimes the best teacher---that's what a number of the people I interviewed made perfectly clear. In fact, when I interviewed Admiral Spane, he was in the process of reading a book about the personal and professional lives of the small number of people who had become five-star admirals. He told me that one of the common themes in each of their careers was that each of them had made some major, potentially career-ending mistakes---but they all got through it. There is hope for the rest of us!

For those of us who are younger, sources of well-intentioned advice sometimes seem endless, and sometimes we just want to be left alone to do our own thing. There are times when we'd rather fail doing it our way, than succeed doing it someone else's way. But, that doesn't mean we are closed off to learning, sometimes the timing just isn't right. If you're reading this book, my guess is the timing might be right for you, right now.

There are a lot of things I plan to do in life, and I have no idea which ones will work out, and which ones won't. I think our job as young people is to keep as many doors of opportunity open, as long as possible, because we never know which one we ultimately may want to enter en route to the next phase of our life. Talking to people who have gone through such "doors" seems well worth our time.

I have been inspired by the wisdom of the people I was able to interview. I hope you have been as well.

I wish you success on your journey, wherever it may take you, and I hope that reading this book has given you some ideas you can use along the way.

About The Author

As this book goes to press, Logan is a senior in high school. He began the quest of setting up interview appointments with highly-successful people when he was 15 years old. He contacted people hoping they would take the time to sit down with him and answer his questions about what advice they could provide to high school and college students for success after graduation. Anyone who knows Logan would not be surprised he would take on a task like this at such a young age.

When he was six years old, he began taking karate lessons. When he was 12, he became one of the youngest black belts in the country. He continued his martial arts training and subsequently became a 2nd degree black belt instructor, and tournament competitor, in Shorin Ryu karate, while also training in boxing and Brazilian Jiu-Jitsu.

Logan also has a tremendous love of cars and airplanes. He cherishes his Mustang, that was largely purchased with money he had saved up from multiple jobs he's had. He participates in all kinds of car-related events including autocross and organized drag racing. In fact, he's such a natural at it that he won first-in-class in his first autocross competition, competing against people were more than twice his age. When time permits, he also takes flying lessons, and is working toward his private pilot's license.

Logan has been fortunate in that he has had the opportunity to travel extensively. He is a keen observer of different cultures and customs and hopes to have the opportunity to study abroad in the next few years.

He enthusiastically looks forward to the college experience, and life beyond college. He knows that he has a few additional tools in his toolbox after having spoken to the wise people he interviewed in this book. He hopes that by sharing what they said with you, that you will also be better prepared for the next phase of your life.

Author Contact Information:

Logan Hensley

Email: turbochargeyourfuture@gmail.com

Acknowledgments

I wish to extend my extreme gratitude to the individuals who allowed me to interview them for this book---Sandy Bauler, Scotty Cameron, John Donahoe, Michael Foss, Tony Hsieh, Frank Naliboff, Ronald Packard, Zerbin Singleton, Robert J. "Rocky" Spane, and Ted Vallas.

When I began this project, I never imagined such accomplished and busy people would take the time to talk with me, a teenager, who just wanted some advice and didn't really know where the project would end up. I learned more than I ever imagined, not only from the interviews themselves, but from seeing how such highly-accomplished and busy people would take the time to help out a young person seeking advice. If I am ever asked to do the same when I'm older, I have learned that I will do exactly the same thing, no matter how busy I am.